This book
is dedicated
to all seekers
of Truth.

Applied Spirituality for bullshit-free living

Text & Illustrations: Mathias Fritzen

Cover in collaboration with: Patricia Sánchez Moreno

Editing: Rebecca Roberts

Proofreading: Patricia Vohwinkel

Independently published 2018

ISBN: 978-1-7266-4310-8

—

Index

TOOLBOX

OUTRO

Preface

»ERZÄHL NICH SON KOKOLORES«

I grew up in a working-class area of Germany with a foundation built on coal-mining and steel-factories. A place where the people are down to earth and practical in their approach to life. Conversation is simple and direct. These are my roots.

If something stinks, you've probably got shit on your shoes. The fastest way to get rid of it is practically, right?

This is what I'm all-in for: Truth without detours. Straightforward and integrated. The end of all bullshit.

This book wrote itself out of joy.

There's a tale of a lion who grew up
in a flock of sheep. After some years,
he ate grass like a sheep and bleated like a sheep.
He didn't know he was a lion.

One day he encountered the lion king who said to him:
»What are you doing here?«
Our little one answered: »Have mercy on me.
Don't eat me. Have mercy on me.«

»Come with me.« the lion king answered
and took him to a lake.

The lion who thought he was a sheep looked into the water
and for the first time he saw his own reflection.
He realized who he really was. He looked to the lion king,
then back to the water again,
and he let out a mighty roar. It took only one brief
moment and he was never a sheep again.

Contrary to popular belief, you are not who you think you are.

You are not...

...your name, age, title or profession.

...your memories or your plans for the future.

...your belief-system, your values or your ideas about life.

...your intelligence, your empathy or your creativity.

...your body, your mind and not even energy.

...your Identified Mind.

You are...

...the absolute Truth of reality.

...THAT from which unconditional Love arises.

...unchanging, timeless, unidentified awareness.

...one with everything and everyone.

...unborn and deathless.

...your Essential Self.

About the Identified Mind
A CONTRACTED VERSION OF YOUR ESSENTIAL SELF

The Identified Mind also goes by the names of ego or person. It is a set of roles, beliefs, concepts, ideas about life and conditioning who you identify with. In Truth you can HAVE all of this but you ARE not it.

Every identification naturally creates a bounding box. It defines the place that you are looking from and lays the foundation for your world-view. If that foundation is not true, literally everything you think, feel or do is built on quicksand. If your ground zero is not zero, your mathematics are preposterous.

The vast majority of the human species today takes one core idea for granted. This idea is

»I am this body and mind.« To believe that you are this little entity, separate from everyone else, is the root cause of all suffering and unconscious behavior that we're witnessing on this planet today. If there's a pull in you to go beyond that, you will need to face the chance of your Identified Mind vanishing.

The perspective that you're most likely looking from at this very moment is the perspective of the Identified Mind. The Identified Mind wants to avoid Self-Realization at all costs. Makes sense! It survives from your attention. What would happen if you remembered your natural freedom and innermost happiness and lose interest in fueling the falsehood?

To believe that you are
this little entity, separate from
everyone else, is the root cause of
all suffering and unconscious
behavior that we're witnessing
on this planet today.

About the Essential Self

THE SUBJECT IN WHICH EVERY OBJECT APPEARS

A thousand pages about honey and you still don't know it's taste. Simply reading about the Essential Self won't do it. Neither will believing in it. The only way to realize who you essentially are is through your own intuitive exploration and direct experience.

Who you are is here, closer than your very breath. How far away from you should it be? Yet, it is so easily overlooked. In a world where everything comes and goes, it is the unchanging. It is beyond name, form and language. It is before the idea of a concept arises. When I tell you that the entire universe appears within you and not you inside the universe, you won't believe me. And you shouldn't! No one can tell

you what Truth is. You have to realize it for yourself – like Buddha, Jesus, Rumi, Anandamayi Ma, Eckhart Tolle, Jim Carrey and maybe the girl next door did before.

There is no need for more head-knowledge, fancy strategies or new belief-systems. What you'll find in this book is simply pointing to a door. You are the one to walk through and experience first hand.

Self-Realization doesn't make you a better person. It simply reveals the Truth about you and reality itself. What you do with it is up to you.

The only way to realize
who you essentially are is through
your own intuitive exploration and
direct experience. What you do
with it is up to you.

All of this has been known for thousands of years –
nothing new. It's time for it to become available
not only for a few, but for everyone.
Become aware of your Identified Mind and its ways.
Discern. Practice. Contemplate. Repeat. Relax back into
the natural freedom and innermost happiness of your
Essential Self. This book is meant to be worked through.
It's meant to challenge you beyond beliefs.
May you discover your Truth and be free.

All this is far out and I lost you? No worries.
We'll slow down. Let me straighten out a few things:
1. The world doesn't need to be saved. It's already safe.
2. You don't need to realize your Essential Self. You are
IT already whether you're aware of it or not. The entire
Journey is an invitation. It is the adventure of a lifetime if
you feel called to take it on. If that is so, two traits have
proven quite useful: Sincerity and devotion.
Here's a great start to empower both. →

Meditation on death
WHATEVER IT TAKES FOR THAT TRUE PATH OF YOURS

I'm throwing some bombs at you right from the start, I know. But what this exercise is really about is compassion. Decide for yourself:

Whether you like it or not, you are going to die. You won't get a prize for your long hours, you can't take your riches with you and even your loved ones face the same destiny. No one ever made it out of here alive. You won't either. It's tempting to push the inevitable away, but let's do the opposite for a moment.

Imagine you're going to die on this exact day and time one year from now. Imagine you're going to die one month from now. One week. Would you still hold grudges? Would you settle for second best? Would you still go for half-assed living? Would you still be doing what you are doing right now? Would you still wait?

Visualize clearly your inevitable death one week from now. Drop over-thinking for a moment and listen to your intuition. For what are you truly here? What is your highest excitement? What would you do to make that happen – to walk that true path of yours?

Whatever your path might be, you've probably just unlocked a good bit of sincerity now. It's time to take responsibility for yourself and make good use of it.

The following chapters all point in the same direction, but from different angles. They are about shifting your vantage point from the Identified Mind towards your Essential Self. There's the opportunity to explore in various depths and with exercises adaptable to your individual needs.

To stay on the surface is optimizing. Diving deeper is liberating. Going all the way may be enlightening.

More explanation:
→ Journey [21]

Start practicing:
→ Intuition [29]

Journey

PERCEIVING FROM CONSCIOUS AWARENESS.
DISSOLVING INTO LOVING PRESENCE.
GROWING UP INSTEAD OF GROWING OLD.

A closer look at the Journey
SHIFTING FROM THE IDENTIFIED MIND TO THE ESSENTIAL SELF

Self-Realization is a Journey, and at the same time it's not. Where do you need to travel in order to find who you really are? How far is that place away from you? Exactly! It has to be right here and now.

This being said, there is a process of remembering and unfolding that is perceived in time. It feels like a Journey that ends where it began – full circle. Totally the same and yet totally different.

Each person goes through a very individual process. There are two dimensions to the Journey that are interlinked but don't necessarily evolve simultaneously for everyone.

1. **The first dimension is the permanent recognition of conscious awareness as your own self.** Many call this an experience of »awakening«, a glimpse of the Truth ultimately leads to an abiding and constant realization. This is what's meant by »shifting from the Identified Mind to the Essential Self«. The place that you're looking out from, your vantage point, changes completely. Everything is seen in a new light. Everything is sparked from a new fire. The ground that you're standing on is unmoving and imperishable. The person that you believed you are is now perceived in front of you. You have an identity, but you are not that. You are the 360° seeing itself.

22

2. **The second dimension is the dissolving of the Identified Mind into loving presence.**

   This is the seeing-through and letting-go-of the illusory nature of what many call ego or person. For very few it happens simultaneously with the perspective-shift that I described as the first dimension. It is an ongoing process, an ever-deepening unfolding. The Identified Mind has the tendency to reassemble itself and knock at your door every once in a while to see if you're still not interested. It is by your vigilance that the Identified Mind dissolves more and more into loving presence, into a so called ego-less state. This is not a state though, it's your natural being.

The experiential realization and embodiment of both these dimensions together is called abiding Self-Realization.

From childhood to adulthood you grow into your identifications. You become someone. That's what people call »growing up«. A strong Identified Mind helps in positioning yourself in society. What's next is growing up from growing up. Astonishingly enough, it means being no one again. This is the real growing up – instead of just growing old.

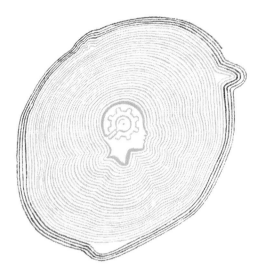

1. Onion layers

One way of visualizing the Journey is the peeling back of the onion layers. Each layer represents a certain aspect of identification that veils who you are at your core. The dents standing for impactful events in your life which created a belief, role or mask.

2. Closing in

Letting go of the outer layers and closing in to the core, the shape of who you really are begins to shine through. Vaguely still, but it's obvious for everyone else (and yourself) now that you are becoming more YOU. These layers represent deeper, earlier layers of conditioning.

3. Sticky bits

Who you really are and how you carry and show yourself is more and more in alignment. Still, there are some sticky bits and pieces that are difficult to see through and let go of. These layers relate to more existential patterns, most coming from early childhood.

4. You

What's left when all the layers have fallen away? You! You've been there all along – at the core of your existence watching this whole process unfold. Now there are no artificial barriers and no boxes that limit your experience. You've rediscovered your natural freedom.

The power of Self-Realization
AND WHAT YOUR IDENTIFIED MIND DOESN'T LIKE ABOUT IT

Self-Realization takes you into the direct experience of who you really are – your Essential Self beyond the Identified Mind.

The Identified Mind is creating the boxes in which you feel stuck – concepts and ideas about life and about yourself that are not real. You unconsciously believe these identifications into existence, and Self-Realization puts an end to that tendency.

The perspective that you're most likely looking from at this very moment is the perspective of the Identified Mind. For this reason it makes a lot of sense that the Identified Mind wants to avoid Self-Realization at all costs!

It will throw at you whatever it takes to distract you from experiencing who you really are. That very experience renders the Identified Mind useless. It leaves you with just you and a perfectly functioning mind that works FOR you not AS you.

The Identified Mind lives from your attention. That is its life force. Once the cord of attention is cut, you're in the process of what is called waking up.

One of the Identified Mind's favorite tricks is that nagging inner voice of criticism: »You're not good enough. You're unworthy. You'll never make it.« and so on. It's perfectly capable of playing a more arrogant role as well: »That's all woo-woo. I see through it easily. I understand it already and there's nothing to learn here.«

It's crucial to be able to discern between the voice of the Identified Mind (which comes from a place of separation, fear and control) and the voice of Intuition (which comes from a place of unity, Love and trust).

Intuition is your compass throughout this whole process. It will guide you to exactly what you need to see in every moment. This is where we begin, diving into the practical chapters and getting clearer one step at a time.

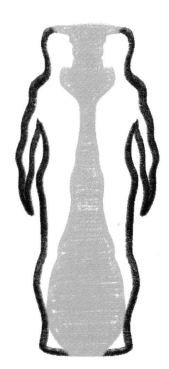

Intuition

NATURALLY NAVIGATING THROUGH LIFE
AND MOVING WITH YOUR OWN FLOW
THROUGH RECONNECTING TO YOUR INNER COMPASS.

Intuitive navigation

TAKING SELF-RESPONSIBILITY TO MOVE WITH YOUR FLOW

The idea »I don't have Intuition« is not true. It's a widespread misconception that some people are intuitive and others are not. There are differences in recognition, but everyone has intuitive capacity!

Think back to an important decision that you made in your life. Can you remember having that deep inner knowing about what's the right way to go for you? You may have pondered the pros and cons, you may have asked people for advice and you may have dismissed your gut-feeling in the end. Still, it was there – that silent whisper within you that knew what was right for you. Do you remember?

Some call it the inner voice or inner compass, some call it a gut-feeling. Pretty much like the GPS in your car, it's your personal navigation system through life as well as through the exercises in this book.

Your »Intuitive Positioning System« (IPS) instinctively understands without the need for rational reasoning. It bridges your conscious and subconscious.

Navigating through life using your Intuition feels natural and effortless. It's flowing with the current. On the contrary, handing over the reigns to your Identified Mind or relying on others has some major side-effects:

- **Rational reasoning**

Everything your Identified Mind knows is accumulated information from the past. The best your mind can create is new interconnections of old information. The content remains stale. Intuition arises from a much greater, much wiser space – fresh in each moment.

- **Asking for advice**

Even the best advice is filtered through the belief-systems, world views and external conditionings of someone else. This person may be an expert in a certain field, but not in your life. You are the expert in your life and Intuition is your tailor-made guiding system.

Now why is this intuitive inner voice so difficult to hear? Simply because there's too much information! There are too many moving pieces battling for your attention. Yet you have the capacity to direct your attention!

Imagine this situation: You're in a crowded café talking to someone you find super interesting. Are you distracted by the noisy café or does the whole world disappear when your attention is focused on this one conversation?

Intuition is a very subtle movement WITHIN you that requires shifting your awareness inwards and away from the large events competing for your attention. Let's visualize this.

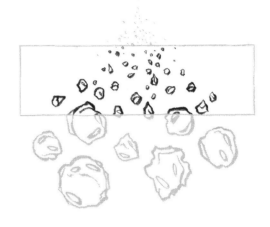

1. Perceptions

On the mission to reconnect to your Intuition the approach is to turn your attention inwards – to shift from the gross to the subtle. You can see, hear, smell, touch and taste. All this noise of sense perceptions has to be seen through.

2. Thoughts

Turning your attention inwards takes it away from sense perception towards your mind. The mind creates an immense amount of noise: Around 50.000 thoughts each day. These thoughts veil your Intuition as well. Further!

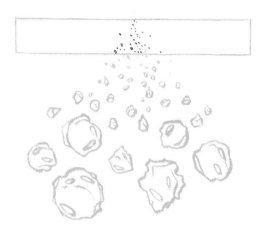

3. Emotions

All emotions spring from thoughts, but they are perceived on a deeper level. Some scream for attention and others are very subtle. Withdrawing attention from even these subtle ones allows you to sense more deeply still.

4. Intuition

Even finer is the quality of Intuition. Metaphorically speaking it's like a diamond floating in an asteroid-belt. Can you keep quiet enough for your attention to pick up on that silent whisper within you? Can you perceive it?

The subtle qualities of Intuition

HOW TO DISCERN BETWEEN INTUITION AND THE IDENTIFIED MIND

The illustrations give an idea of the nature of Intuition, but how to discern whether something is an intuitive hit or mere mind-chatter?

Intuition shows up differently from person to person. Some literally hear a voice speaking. Some see color, others just experience a knowingness. Regardless of the channel, there are certain general qualities to Intuition.

1. **Intuition is not rational**

   It may point you in directions that are contrary to how you think life should be. Maybe you can't find rational reasons for it and you can't explain it, but the intuitive hit still feels right for you.

2. **Intuition inexplicably knows more**

   As Intuition is connected with deeper layers of yourself, it has access to much more information than your Identified Mind. Even if you're not aware yet, it knows what you need to experience next.

3. **Intuition doesn't argue**

   It suggests and gives you free reign over the next steps to take. It is not invested in the outcome and has no need to justify itself. It won't shout to get its point across.

4. **Intuition doesn't come with an action-plan**

   It doesn't lay out to-dos, milestones or an overview of the situation. Even if you ask why it suggests a certain direction, it will not provide an overview. If there's an answer to your why-question, it comes from your Identified Mind.

5. Intuition has a lightness to it

It is not the fearful voice of a scared child. Neither is it screaming aggressively like a choleric. It has an air of deep wisdom. It can still be persistent, but in a gentle way.

6. Intuition doesn't care about your plans

Your meticulous mind-made plans for the future don't matter. From Intuition's vantage point they are seen through and replaced by what really matters to you.

You get a sense that Intuition can collide quite severely with your rationality. It is also because of this collision that you're naturally prone to dismiss intuitive insights. If it doesn't suit your plans you will discard it. That's OK, of course. If it is substantial, it will raise its hand again anyway.

Until you can distinguish Intuition from mind-chatter and experience that Intuition is always right, you won't be able to fully let go into its flow.

That may need some practice.

Calibrating your IPS

Each chapter in this book contains a section like this where practical exercises are suggested to explore a certain pointer. These exercises are very specific and easily applicable.

You are explicitly invited to modify each exercise to fit your own needs. Combine exercises in new ways or invent your own.

Since we're focused on Intuition, I'd suggest following your gut-feeling during these exercises as well. Hone your Intuition on a daily basis to cultivate that inner connection. Play with it and build trust until it becomes totally natural to be tuned into it.

1

Brain dump
BYPASSING MENTAL PATTERNS

Choose a topic that holds weight for you. Grab paper and pen and set a timer for 10 minutes. **Write down whatever comes to mind – no editing, no judgment. The pen doesn't stop moving even if it's writing »bla bla«.** Let it sit for a while. Revisit with fresh eyes and give space for surprising (even odd) insights to show up. What sticks out from the text-cloud?

Give in to the flow
INTUITIVE MOVEMENT

2

Retreat into a quiet room at home, close the door and shutters, switch off your phone. Sit for a while and feel what arises in the moment. You can close your eyes. **Put on some music that feels evocative and start moving. Don't try to move in a specific way, just move freely. Let it flow.** No one is there to judge you. There's just sound and your intuitive expression.

Guided city tour
THE ART OF HAVING NO PLAN

3

Take an afternoon off and head out to the city center. A bigger city works best. Now that you're here, start moving. No phones or maps allowed. Don't look at roadsigns. Just move intuitively, guided by your inner compass. **Take turns, go slow or fast, sit down, talk to someone... everything is allowed that feels intuitively right for you. Discover the city like a child.**

Notes and reflections

Use this section for the »Brain dump« exercise. Reflect on challenges you're facing in everyday-life related to your Intuition.

»I got it, but...« — Common blocks

»If I followed what my Intuition suggests, the whole world would turn against me. It's so counterintuitive to the ideas of my friends and families... what to do?«

»I feel totally in tune with my Intuition and my life flows naturally with it. The problem is that I find myself unable to plan anything anymore.«

Throughout this whole book you'll find pointers towards self-responsibility. This is a good example. It's your life and you're the expert in it. Ask yourself what you truly want. **If there was only one thing that you can ask for, what would it be? If that one thing turned the whole world against you, would you chose to be a sheep or a lion?** You've got plenty of time to figure it out. Life is endlessly patient.

We've compared Intuition with a GPS, like a navigation tool. The rational mind works like a calculator, your tool for planning. You have both tools available at all times. There is no need to fire one and hire the other. To book a flight and a hotel for your holidays requires some rationality for planning. Let Intuition select the destination and you'll find a natural balance.

»There is a decision I must make, and it will hurt someone's feelings. I know intuitively that it's the right move. What do I do?«

Intuition won't suggest harm but it may suggest a move that dispels illusions. For example, perhaps you hold onto a concept of a relationship, but in truth it makes you unhappy. Intuition may give certain hints. Ultimately deciding to let go of a relationship that is only held together by concepts is healing, but it may create momentary suffering. That does not mean the movement is wrong.

Got a burning question? Send an email to
Book@MathiasFritzen.com

This is how the chapters flow.

Test your intuition and go through them following your own order.

What speaks to you first?
Start there!

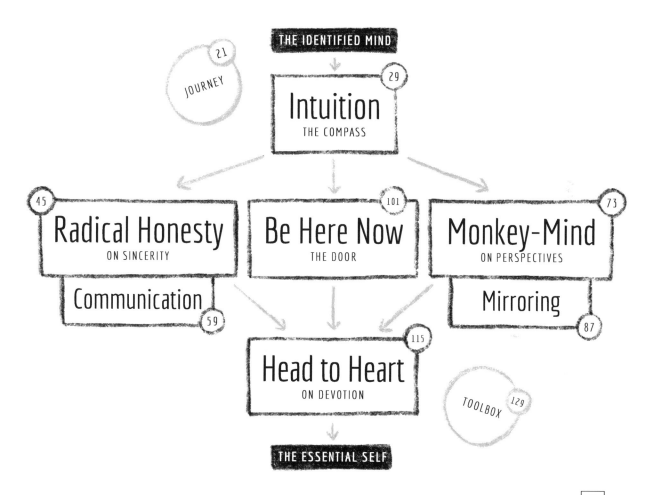

THE IDENTIFIED MIND

21
JOURNEY

Intuition
THE COMPASS
29

Radical Honesty
ON SINCERITY
45

Be Here Now
THE DOOR
101

Monkey-Mind
ON PERSPECTIVES
73

Communication
59

Mirroring
87

Head to Heart
ON DEVOTION
115

TOOLBOX
129

THE ESSENTIAL SELF

43

44

Radical Honesty

EXPRESSING YOUR OWN TRUTH
AND LIVING WITHOUT MASKS AND ROLES
THROUGH DITCHING STRESSFUL FALSE IDENTITIES.

The way into the real world
PLAY AND PITFALLS OF THE IDENTIFIED MIND

It's your birthday and you have a mix of friends and family over for the party. As you stroll around you pick up on a conversation between your partner, a good friend and an old colleague. They're talking about the trouble you had at work last week and they seem to disagree over some facts. That's when it hits you: All of them know a different version of the story and now the stories are colliding.

You've filtered and edited bits and pieces, wrapping it all up in neat, digestible packages tailored to each individual. Now you feel the different worlds collapsing into each other. How to get out of this? Tell the truth? Distract? Run away?

Does this situation sound familiar?

It illustrates a common tendency of the Identified Mind. **To identify with certain roles and secure the status quo of those roles involves clever tweaks to the true story – sometimes even blatant lies and fabrications.**

That's how the Identified Mind tries to preserve control. It requires meticulous work to maintain how it wants to be perceived: By co-workers, friends, partner, family and strangers.

Good that you're not the Identified Mind! Can you dare to bring yourself to everyone without editing?

If you find yourself being heavily identified with certain roles, your life may feel:

- **Stressful and exhausting**
  It requires a huge amount of energy to maintain false identities. This is especially true when you change quickly between roles and situations, or when various versions of yourself crash into each other.

- **Misaligned and separated**
  False identities attract people and life-situations that match to the false identity you project and not to you who you really are. What you truly desire will not come if you don't show yourself fully and authentically.

- **Locked-up and limited**
  By showing up as you think you should, you silently agree with a system of restrictions, limitations and boundaries. You literally co-create the constipated system that keeps you boxed in.

Since you are beyond any of these false identities, you also have the power to release them. Great news, right?

Before proceeding to the how-to's, let's visualize how this whole masking system plays out and ultimately separates us from each other.

1. People play roles

You don't see others as they authentically are. You see the version of them that they present to you. You see the illusion that they want you to see. You see the masks they wear and the roles they play.

2. You play roles

Are you the same person with your partner, friends and colleagues? You've been taught to protect yourself, to fit in or standout, to avoid complications and confrontation. The result: You are not seen for who you authentically are.

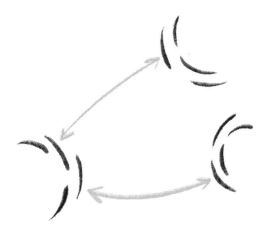

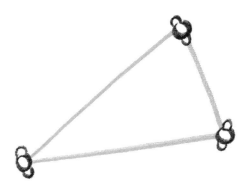

3. Roles meet roles

When everyone plays their habitual roles in various situations and walks of life, we end up in a fake world. No one really sees anyone. False identities are communicating and interacting with other false identities.

4. Authentic meeting

Radical Honesty allows for authentic meetings. Expressing and showing up as you truly are is a powerful invitation for others to do the same: »I'm unarmed. Meet me here in this open space.«

How Radical Honesty serves you

EXPRESSING YOUR OWN TRUTH

Radical Honesty allows for authentic meetings. OK, but what does Radical Honesty even mean? We can say that it stands for:

Fundamentally facing what's going on within yourself without trying to manipulate or distort. In other words, Radical Honesty is quite literally the expression of your natural being.

It requires no additional energy to be authentic. You are just you. All the time. No need to memorize ever-complicated cascades of stories. No longer feeling tight-chested in difficult situations. No longer making tiptoe-responses. No need to prepare for social situations. What a relief!

In simply being yourself, you begin to attract, that which you truly desire. It may look quite different from what you imagined, but many of life's most auspicious gifts come in surprising packages.

Once you've discovered the simplicity and ease of Radical Honesty, it starts to create a vacuum. In giving space to yourself, you create space for others to be who they truly are as well.

It no longer makes sense for others to play out their false identities in your presence because, in the most compassionate way, you're not interested in their stories. You're genuinely interested in THEM.

Radical Honesty within yourself and towards others eventually dissolves the fictional self-images that separate you from reality. Some other side effects are:

1. **Significant stress-reduction**
2. **Massive boosts in energy**
3. **Deepening relationships**

4. **Freedom from previous conditioning**
5. **Attracting what you truly want**
6. **Comfort with yourself**

7. **Decreasing judgments**
8. **Decreasing biases**
9. **Clarity**

A few last things before we head into application: Remember that you are in charge! There are no should-dos or have-tos in true self-responsibility.

There is no limit to Radical Honesty. This is why it's called radical. There is always room to deepen and explore further.

Stay vigilant! Don't THINK about what is relevant for you and what is not. Intuitively FEEL into it – deeply, you know it already.

Practicing Radical Honesty

To understand and embody Radical Honesty it's important to look at the play between inside and outside. Radical Honesty always begins with yourself: What do I think, what do I feel, what drives me, what are my desires and what lies in my subconscious shadows?

Only after facing this first step can you start to share your insights with others. Radical Honesty is absolutely not just tied to the negative! »Being around you gives me a lot of energy.« or »I really appreciate your creative ideas.« are examples for honest statements that many don't dare to speak out loud.

Now let's jump into something practical.

1

Honesty protocol
TAKING THE FIRST STEPS

Shift your attention inside towards your hidden thoughts and feelings. Take time to write and reflect on your self-judgments and explore what comes up. Start by taking notes on the following questions:

• Of what am I afraid or ashamed?
• For what am I waiting and why?
• What am I avoiding at all costs?

Judgment circle
CREATING SPACE FOR HONESTY

Create a safe and quiet space to sit down with a trusted friend or family member. Take time to settle in and make yourselves comfortable. Now with compassion but without filter:

1. **Exchange what you cannot stand or even hate about each other.**
2. **Exchange what you absolutely love or admire about each other.**

Enter the fray
FACING AVOIDANCE STRATEGIES

As you grow more comfortable being honest with yourself and others, you can begin to amp it up. **Pick someone to whom you avoid speaking at all costs. The conversation you don't dare to have but you feel the urge to finally face.** Center yourself and speak your truth from the heart – vulnerability helps. Keep having these meetings!
→ See chapter on Communication [59]

Notes and reflections

Use this section for your »Honesty protocol«. As well take notes on blocks that come up being radically honest within yourself and towards others.

»I got it, but...« — Common blocks

»Does being radically honest mean that I should share everything that I feel and think about with everyone?«

»I'm having trouble identifying what I truly want behind all these roles and masks. Who am I if all of them fall away?«

No. Radical Honesty means to get rid of internal filters to see things as they are within yourself, without bias or judgment. This is the neutral ground. From here you still have the choice of what to share and what not. There is no standard solution. You will intuitively know what is relevant in each situation.

→ See chapter on Intuition [29]

→ See chapter on Communication [59]

Stick with the exercise »Honesty protocol« for a while and **carve out a week of time where you put yourself first. During this time you only do what you want.** No looking outside of yourself. No compromise. If you cannot think of anything that you want, simply move! Do something you used to love in the past or try out new things, but keep moving and checking in with yourself: Does this resonate with me?

»It's difficult enough to admit what I truly think and feel within myself, but I'm completely lacking the courage to share it with others.«

It might be tough to admit, but if you're lacking courage, perhaps you're not tired enough of the roles-game. Maybe it needs to be played out for a little while longer. That's fine, too. No worries! **When you're totally fed up with the game, the courage for change will naturally arise. All the energy required for your next big leap is already available.** Truly, motivation or encouragement is not needed.

Got a burning question? Send an email to
Book@MathiasFritzen.com

Communication

BECOMING GENTLE IN SELF-TALK
AND SHARING FROM YOUR CENTER
THROUGH RELEASING JUDGMENTS ON YOURSELF AND OTHERS.

Communicating is relating
AND LANGUAGE IS QUITE AN INACCURATE TOOL

Life is relationship. You are in relationship with every person that you meet, with every object that you touch and, even before that, you are in relationship with yourself!

Relationship literally means relating and connecting to something or someone. Whether it's internal thoughts or externally verbalized, as soon as we relate to something or someone we start communicating.

Communication impacts relationships both, at work and in private life, and it can play a powerful role in your journey towards Self-Realization. So let's start at the origin: How do you talk with yourself?

Most people manage to be outwardly polite and genuine but are absolutely ruthless in their self-talk. That's where the Identified Mind excels: criticism, perfectionism, control, doubt and exaggeration.

Your internal Communication – self-talk – massively influences your external Communication. A good listener can pick up on what your self-talk may be like by just listening to your conversations with others.

In the same way, judgments you may have about others are carried over from your internal Communication to the outside. Your Identified Mind finds subtle ways to sneak them in.

Communication happens inside, outside and in between. It's a bridge, but not a stable one.

Across the world more than 7.000 different languages are spoken. All of them are simplified sets of symbols to describe what we perceive. All of them are inaccurate by their very nature. **Language is amazing, yes. But there is plenty of room for misunderstanding, and it's quite useful to simply be aware of that fact.**

Have you ever witnessed two people speaking about two completely different topics, but both thinking that the other is following and understanding? That's not a rare case! How much of what we want to convey is really understood?

This is especially true with conversations that are emotionally charged. Often these talks repeat again and again – leading to a dead end. When this cycle has repeated itself often enough, we tend to avoid the confrontations altogether.

What usually happens is that unconscious patterns are triggered due to miscommunication and the discussion becomes emotional, leading to a debate on principles.

How is it possible to overcome this trap? First, let's look at some common tendencies.

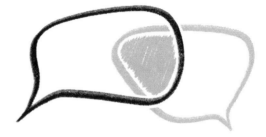

1. Self-talk

You are your own worst critic. How you talk to yourself defines how you approach others. Where do you criticize yourself? In which areas do you have self-doubts? Can you accept yourself exactly the way you are right now?

2. Judgments

Judgments regarding others are a strategy of the Identified Mind to create separation where there is none. Someone else is neither better nor worse, above or below you. In reality, we are all equal. Inquire into your judgments!

3. Crossing the line

The circles represent a person's »I-zone« where individuals are staying with themselves. When you step over into another person's zone, you speak FOR them. This creates a high potential for negative reactivity.

4. Centered sharing

As you become more aware of your own inner world (mastering self-talk and judgments) and begin sharing your perceptions from a place of vulnerability, you will invite others to do the same. This is centered sharing and it's contagious.

Self-responsibility and new perspectives
THE WAY TO CENTERED SHARING

Centered sharing is really an inside-out approach. A great place to begin with is becoming aware of your self-talk. It's astonishing how harshly we judge ourselves and others. Becoming more gentle in your self-talk and releasing judgments on others is the foundation for the following two approaches on responsible external Communication.

1. Sharing from the I-Perspective

Stay in your I-zone! As soon as you accuse, assume or generalize, you overstep someone else's zone. An easy way to avoid this is simply by communicating strictly from a vulnerable I-Perspective. Here are a few examples to illustrate the do's and don'ts:

✘ You're thoughtless! Because of you I have to take care of everything.

✓ **I feel left out and the responsibility that I take on feels like a burden.**

✘ That's mean! Why do you make me feel this way?

✓ **I'm hurt and I feel sad. I would like to better understand the situation.**

✘ This is clearly your fault! You only seem to care about yourself.

✓ **I feel left out and I would like to be appreciated and seen for who I am.**

I think this. I feel that. It sounds almost too simple, but it's miraculous. By leaving out accusations and staying on your side of the conversation, you will remove the energetic charge that often leads to misunderstandings and arguments.

2. Sharing from the Meta-Perspective

In order to remain with yourself you need to be aware of what you think and feel. What's actually going on within you in any given situation? When you shift into observing yourself, you can vulnerably share what you perceive from that witnessing place. This requires courage and trust, but it's highly rewarding! Here are a few examples:

✓ To be honest... right now... I feel very insecure and vulnerable. I'm afraid to make a mistake. I would like to take some space and breathing room.

✓ Can I share something with you? I feel very low on energy right now and I would like to be more present in this discussion. How would it feel for you to continue later?

✓ It would be a great relief to find clarity, but for now I feel confused and overwhelmed. I would love for you to help me sort through this if you're up for it.

Let's talk!

Gentle self-talk, non-judgment and vulnerable sharing from the two new perspectives give a significantly greater chance of more productive and positive Communication.

This comes in handy as you dig deeper into the chapter on → Radical Honesty [45].

The result is that your inner and outer Communication collapses into one harmonized language. What a relief! You don't need to worry how to say certain things or feel the need to shy away from difficult situations.

Let's start from the inside-out again.

Truce
BEFRIENDING YOURSELF

What are the worst things that you tell yourself in your inner dialogue? Write them down, unfiltered. Now say out loud in direct-speech what you wrote down and record it. Play it back and ask yourself:

1. Would I ever tell anyone else the things I'm saying to myself?
2. How can I choose to treat myself more gently from now on?

1

Judgment antidote
DEVELOPING A NEW HABIT

2

There is a tendency of the Identified Mind to focus on what's better, worse or different about others when we first meet them. Practice the opposite: Focus on similarities! **Focus on things you have in common and what aspects you share. How does this person remind you of yourself?** How are you alike? In doing this you actively choose to close the gap of separation.

Break the cycle
OPENING UP FRESH PERSPECTIVES

3

Break the cycle of an emotionally-charged conversation that repeats again and again using the two methods: I-Perspective and Meta-Perspective. Even if it feels odd, stick strictly with the two methods at first to avoid falling back into old patterns. You can also inform your partner about what you're exactly doing – that's part of the Meta-Perspective.

Notes and reflections

Use this section for the »Truce« exercise. Reflect on difficult conversations that you're having and identify where you left your zone.

»I got it, but...« — Common blocks

»I just can't stop my negative self-talk. It's so much easier for me to focus on others and meet them in a compassionate way.«

»I wasn't even aware that I constantly judge, label and categorize people. Is there another way to stop that?«

Most likely some of these negative thought-patterns were established early on in your life. **As shown in the Journey chapter, these are the deeper layers of the onion and they can be quite sticky. Don't force it.** Part of being gentle with yourself is accepting these negative thoughts instead of pushing them away.

→ See chapter on Head to Heart [115]

Looking up to someone or down on someone is a natural tendency of the Identified Mind. It wants to position itself in society. **One way to counter that habit is not to try to stop it. Sit back and observe the automated movements of the mind.** As you relax back into this observer place, you're no longer the thinker of your thoughts and become the detached witness.

→ See chapter on the Monkey-Mind [73]

»Somehow I'm constantly trying to mind-read others to find out what they want from me. Anticipation is how I try to avoid hurting someone.«

You're altering your Communication based on assumptions. The truth is, you can't mindread. You're just moving the conversation to an abstract level instead of a natural one. **Self-responsibility comes first. What do you think and feel? Communicate that unfiltered. In doing so you give space for others to do the same.**

→ See chapter on Be Here Now [101]
→ See chapter on Mirroring [87]

Got a burning question? Send an email to
Book@MathiasFritzen.com

Monkey-Mind

TAKING THE DETACHED OBSERVER-SEAT
AND SHIFTING FROM TUNNEL-VISION TO BIRD'S EYE VIEW
THROUGH DISENTANGLING FROM YOUR MONKEY-MIND.

Jumping and jabbering non-stop

DISENTANGLING FROM YOUR MONKEY-MIND

Imagine a little monkey who's trying to catch your attention. He's shifting from side to side and jumping up and down. He's making faces and stages great drama, mixing it up with unexpected moves and strange sounds. **All that just so you stay absorbed in his grand show. The monkey sits in your Identified Mind and your attention is his reward.**

Every time you give him attention it reinforces a certain amount of belief in the thoughts he's throwing at you. It makes them feel so real that most people are fully identified with their thinking. How to stop this? To answer that question we first have to investigate if there's something more behind the thought-layer.

Thoughts are the monkey's ammunition and you have around 50.000 of them everyday. Funny though, that a day has 86.400 seconds. So not every second is filled with a thought. What happens in between? Are you gone? No, you're still here. That's good news! You happen to have thoughts but you are not your thoughts. Thoughts are like passing clouds. You see them coming and going and you have the choice to follow them or let them go. Somehow there must be a space from which you're able to watch your thoughts passing. Are there more hints that this space exists?

I remember walking to the train station after a party. My friend said with remarkable clarity:

»Wow, I'm so drunk. That's crazy. I wonder if I can make it home«. Who is talking about who there? Is the one that perceives the drunk-body drunk himself? An observation that is so clear – where does it come from in that moment? The space from which the observation comes seems to be clearly detached from the body.

Here's another one: My grandma had dementia and used to say: »When I was younger I was able to remember everything. Now my memory is not working anymore.«. Again, who is making a statement like that? Not the one that suffers from dementia, right? The space from which the observation comes seems to have vast overview beyond the Identified Mind.

There must be an observer within us who perceives these things without being involved in them.

Taking the observer-seat is what this whole chapter is about. It disentangles you from the identification with your Monkey-Mind. We can say it re-establishes you as the CEO of your life and your Monkey-Mind as your employee – restoring the natural order.

The hot air balloon is a nice metaphor to visualize how drastically your vantage point influences life experiences.

1. Ground level

Imagine you're downtown in a big city in the middle of the everyday buzz. There's the noise of the traffic, people having phone-calls rushing by and flashy advertisements grabbing for your attention. This is the view of the Identified Mind.

2. Leaving the buzz

You're embarking on a hot-air balloon, gently rising above the many rooftops. The noise fades out. The busy people look somewhat cute from up here. It's easier to breathe. You are shifting into observer-mode.

3. Bird's-eye view

The first fleecy clouds appear around you and some birds are passing by. What was previously overwhelming down there in the city feels like play now. From this detached place everything becomes light and clear.

4. Above the clouds

Even the clouds are seen now. It's very quiet up here. A gentle warm breeze of fresh air and a stunning view. You can rest now. This is pure witnessing. The Identified Mind and its ways don't affect you.

From tunnel vision to bird's-eye view

TAKE THE OBSERVER-SEAT AND ENJOY PURE WITNESSING

From the perspective of a hot-air balloon, even the worst traffic jam looks peaceful and serene. Pretty much in the same way **you can practice watching your thoughts instead of getting involved in them. The disentangling happens simply in the act of observing!**

What happens for many people is this: They are absolutely fed up with the monkey, or perhaps it goes even further than that: They are on substantial medication because the turmoil created by the constant mind-chatter has become unbearable. Now the natural impulse is wanting to make the monkey stop. Simply make him shut up and keep quiet. Often that draws people to meditation.

Now when you make efforts to stop something that lives ONLY by your attention, guess what will happen. It'll get worse! The monkey sits in your Identified Mind and your Identified Mind only comes into existence through you. It has no inherent reality to it. Any time you believe in one of the monkeys tricks it's like trying to extinguish fire with alcohol – you fuel it even more.

Watch your thoughts, that's all. The disentangling happens simply in the act of watching. It sounds strange but that's the whole secret. Thoughts are coming and going like passing clouds. No matter how awe-inspiring or terrifying they are, you watch them from the detached place of an observer. Stay as a clean witness who is not involved in the drama. As soon as you become aware of your own involvement, watch that, too!

1. Insomnia, stress and physical illness are often the consequences of constant mind-chatter endured for decades. Observing the Monkey-Mind creates the space that's needed for healing. Beyond that: It reminds you of a space within yourself that is already sane and whole.

2. When you find that you behave in the same way over and over again it may indicate a conditioned behavior-pattern.

Every pattern that you have can be observed, revealed and done away with if desired. Again the most important step is to become aware of the patterns by observing what's going on within you.

Our bodies can be drunk, yes. Our brains can suffer from dementia, yes. We can have the wildest and most dreadful thoughts coming up, yes. But our inner observer is neither drunk nor sick, neither guilty of thinking nor clinging to any wishful idea.

To observe means to become aware. Being aware is what creates choice. Choice is freedom and that's the fragrance of your Essential Self.

Relaxing back into spacious silence

Remember the illustrative journey – from ground-level towards bird's-eye view? That's what the Monkey-Mind practice is about.

First disentangling through increased awareness of your thoughts and then relaxing back more and more into the spaciousness of pure witnessing. Uninvolved and detached observing without labeling, judging or anticipating. All that arises is thought and can be watched as well. How far can you go back? How subtle can your perception become?

The quality of silence reveals itself the more you stop trying. The ultimate observer is the place you're looking from – your Essential Self.

Tuning in
EXITING THE TUNNEL

1

It can be tricky to get your feet off the ground at first. One way to do it is to **take down short notes on the thoughts you see arising within you like this: »Grandma. Stress. Kids. Groceries. Pink. Warm. Joy. Plans...«** Do this in a daily 10-minute session to hone your awareness. Create space between you as the observer and your thoughts.

Lie in ambush
EXTENDING THOUGHT-BREAKS

86.400 seconds a day and only 50.000 thoughts. That's one thought every 1,7 seconds. **To extend the break in between you have to lie in ambush! Focus all your attention as if your life depends on it and wait for the next thought to arise.** Don't miss it! You have to be attentive to an extent that you are there before the next thought arises. Maxed out alertness required.

2

33 minutes
BECOMING THE OBSERVER

Sit in silence for just 11 minutes. Don't worry about your posture, just sit comfortably and don't fall asleep. Your only task is to watch your thoughts without labeling, judging or getting involved. When you get carried away, gently bring your attention back to observing. Work your way up to 3 of these sessions every day: Morning, lunchbreak and before going to bed.

3

Notes and reflections

Use this section for the »Tuning in« exercise. Isn't it fascinating what your monkey comes up with? Are you really the one who makes all this up?

»I got it, but...« — Common blocks

»I think I'm totally lost in my thoughts.
I don't know where to even start.«

»I became aware of the watcher.
Now I'm watching the watcher, but this
one can also be observed. It's an endless
succession!«

**The question »where to start« is a thought
that arises within your Identified Mind.** As
you become aware of it, right now it is clearly
an object of your perception. You see it. It's in
front of you. You are not this thought. In the
same way, every other thought is an object that
you can perceive. The more this sinks in, the
more distance between you and your thoughts
is created. You have already begun.

**The idea of an infinite loop is in itself a trap of
the Identified Mind. The succession is finite:**
There is thought (Identified Mind) and there's
the observing »I«. This I is itself observed
from a non-personal space of pure awareness
(Essential Self). That space is absolute without
anything »behind« it. This becomes clear in
direct experience. Stay vigilant to the tricks of
your mind. You're always one step ahead!

»I observe everything but that leaves me totally detached from the world. I feel somewhat removed and high up. I can't relate to anyone anymore.«

Why are you hanging out in the hot-air balloon? It is an excursion that provides you with the overview of a fresh perspective. **You're safe to come down to ground-level again with your new found insights and clarity. Try out your realization in the marketplace!** If you get lost again: Back to observing. If you feel content, that's a sign of a certain amount of embodiment. Witnessing happens on all levels!

Got a burning question? Send an email to
Book@MathiasFritzen.com

Mirroring

OUTPLAYING YOUR IDENTIFIED MIND
AND BECOMING WHO YOU REALLY ARE
THROUGH TRACING BACK AND EXPOSING YOUR MIRRORS.

Talking about yourself, are you?

SEEING THROUGH THE GAME OF YOUR IDENTIFIED MIND

A collection of concepts and ideas about life and about yourself that is not real, conditioning that you picked up on from your parents, friends and role-models – all of these make up your Identified Mind.

If that's the case, and if the perspective you're looking from at this very moment is the perspective of the Identified Mind, then there must be traces of the Identified Mind in everything you think or say, right? You've just discovered a very effective loophole enabling you to see through the game. It's called Mirroring.

When you THINK about yourself and others – does it reflect reality as it truly is or do you have biases, judgments, expectations, assumptions and interpretations that may derive from your Identified Mind?

How is it when you TALK about yourself and others? Does it reflect reality as it is or can you sense your Identified Mind there as well?

What we usually don't want to admit is that what we think or say is a direct reflection back to ourselves.

Look into the mirror with compassion and face what's there. In doing so you discern what is true and what is not, systematically dissolve personal blocks one at a time.

The bits and pieces of your Identified Mind that can be found in your thinking and talking have a certain feel that helps identifying them. On the head-level we can call it narrow-minded. On the level of the body it's a contraction in the gut. Energetically speaking, it's heavy and negative or unsettled and angry. In terms of self-perception it's either a sense of superiority or a sense of unworthiness. All of this reveals the Identified Mind. It's trigger-energy that can be seen and converted into positive, expansive energy. You get the idea.

Again: Everything that you think or say is tagged by the place that it comes from – your Identified Mind or your Essential Self.

Mirroring plays out all the time. In your everyday-life you can learn plenty from it. The first step is becoming aware of it, which has already begun. This awareness seeps through into deeper and deeper layers and becomes finer and finer. Observing needs to be intentionally at first and becomes more natural as the muscle is flexed. The process continues to deepen as long as the mirror needs to be polished.

Let's shine some light on the different forms and expressions of Mirroring in detail.

1. In interactions

When you're speaking with someone and you listen to yourself talking – do you sound like one of your parents sometimes? Do you impose your own ideas on others? Can you sense your Identified Mind within your statements?

2. In observations

When no one is listening, your identified mind has much less restraint. While you are observing a scene, a conversation or someone passing by – can you hear the many judgments your Identified Mind comes up with?

3. In self-talk

How is it when no one is around? What are your first thoughts about the world and about yourself right after you wake up? Are there repetitive thought-patterns and conditioning speaking, or is what you think fresh?

4. Polished mirror

When there is no trace of your Identified Mind to be found in your inner and outer conversations, the mirror has been polished. It is no longer obscured and reflects reality as it is without interference. Polishing needs vigilance.

The place you're communicating from

EVERYDAY-LIFE EXAMPLES AND THEIR MIRRORED-MEANINGS

Mirroring is a form of self-inquiry that can be hard to grasp at first. After all, you're questioning something that you have taken for granted for most of your life: Yourself.

If a mirror is clean and well polished, it only reflects what stands in front of it. Are you seeing a direct reflection of what's really in front of you or are you seeing some part of yourself reflected back? Have a close look and investigate in your everyday interactions. Who is thinking? Who is talking? How does this one perceive the world? Is this really you?

Let's have a look at some examples and their possible mirrored-meanings:

1. In interactions

I say: »Put on some clothes, it's cold outside!«
I mean: I feel cold and want to put on some clothes myself if I go outside.

I say: »Mind your own business!«
I mean: You hit on something that triggers me and I don't want to expose it.

I say: »You should definitely talk about it.«
I mean: I should talk about it and I'd like for you to go ahead and test the waters.

I say: »You feel cold and distanced today.«
I mean: I feel disconnected from you and my own emotions. I distance myself.

2. In observations

I think: »Look at that couple kissing in public...
how awkward. They should get a room.«
I mean: I'm afraid to embrace or express my
own intimacy or sexuality in public.

I think: »There she is... I expected her to dress
provocatively like that. Shameful!«
I mean: I'm worried how others perceive me
and what their opinions are.

I think: »Dirty train station... only fat people
here... and the pigeons are disgusting.«
I mean: It's hard to meet my own narrow defini-
tions of what's acceptable and what not.

3. In self-talk

I think: »I only have superficial conversations
with superficial people.«
I mean: I don't see my capability to create
inspiring conversations.

I think: »My life is just the same... day in day
out. It's like in Groundhog Day.«
I mean: I'm not being self-responsible creating
what I wish to experience.

I think: »No one called me lately. I bet it will be
the exact same today.«
I mean: I prepare myself to suffer and indulge
victim-hood instead of taking action myself.

Polishing the mirror

I've seen it many times that, after very little practice, people become aware of how they are reflecting themselves on their surroundings. Mid-sentence they suddenly pause and reflect: »OK, I'll keep that one for myself. It's solely about me and not about them.«

It's frustrating and fun at the same time to polish your mirror. It leads to not believing your own thoughts anymore, and that's a good thing! It leads to discovering the very source of your thoughts. What is the nature of the one who's thinking these thoughts? How does he see the world? Is she influenced and conditioned, transient or steady? That's the door to liberation.

Judgment journal
UNCOVERING CONDITIONING

1

Note down judgments that you have on others and inquire what they tell you about yourself. Are you judging the same tendency within yourself? Are you envious of this expression and don't allow yourself to open up to it? Who's having these judgments – you or your parents? Where did you pick them up? This inquiry trains your awareness of your mirrors.

Self-inquiry
TRACING THE ROOT-THOUGHT

2

Become aware of what you say. **Once you identify something that could be a mirror, trace it back to its source. What is the root-thought behind it?** Is it really true? Are you 100% certain that this is true? What's the worldview behind this thought? Finding these root-thoughts and compassionately looking at them will naturally begin to dissolve them.

Game of mirrors
THE FAST LANE

3

Find yourself an accountability partner who is into spiritual practice as well. **Mutually agree on calling each other out any time you sense a mirror.** Whenever you feel that the other person is actually talking about her- or himself: »Mirror!« Fair warning, this can be highly annoying, but it's also very effective in boosting awareness.

Notes and reflections

Use this section for the »Judgment journal« and »Self-inquiry«. Everything that you think or say is about yourself, but from which part?

»I got it, but...« — Common blocks

»I'm confused. Somehow I don't get this whole Mirroring thing. I don't see my mirrors. Can you help me?«

»OK, I see mirrors everywhere now, but what to do with them? How can I get rid of them?«

Identifications shape a person. When I was working in digital design I had a constant loop running in my head that was judging on the usability and looks of any website or app that I saw. A constant judgment-pattern that was of high importance to me at that time, hence being identified as a sophisticated designer. **What are you identified with? Are you thinking and speaking from the place of identification?**

Holding them in loving awareness is enough. Your awareness is broadening more and more and you're conscious of your mirrors now. That's great! The question at this point is not what to do with them, but more what not to do with them. Now that you are aware – would you choose to act these mirrors out? Would you choose to accuse someone of something that's actually about yourself?

»I see so many mirrors in other people. They think they talk about me, but it's about themselves. Should I tell them and how?«

Unasked advice is like bragging – nobody likes it. **If your wish to share comes from a place of compassion, you could ask permission to share your observations. If they're OK with it, go ahead.** But keep in mind: It was your wish to share in the first place, not their wish to know. The communication-technique sharing from the I-perspective applies well here!

→ See chapter on Communication [59]

Got a burning question? Send an email to
Book@MathiasFritzen.com

Be Here Now

CUTTING OUT DISTRACTIONS
AND BREAKING THE CYCLE OF YOUR MIND WANDERING OFF
THROUGH BEING FULLY INVOLVED WITH WHAT IS.

The illusion of time

NOTHING EVER HAPPENS OUTSIDE OF THE PRESENT MOMENT

Time does not exist. It is a concept that enables us to refer to certain events and put them into context. Experientially speaking there is never anything happening outside of the present moment.

Have you ever experienced anything in the past or will you ever experience anything in the future? In reality it is impossible to escape the eternal now. In virtuality however, it is very well possible to reminisce and to project.

Every memory and all imaginings are virtual. They are thoughts existing only inside your Identified Mind as illusory bubbles shrouding the here and now.

»Live in the moment!« – I bet you've heard or read this advice many times. The crucial question is: How do I live in the moment?

Many of us are habitually escaping life in our compulsive thinking. In doing so we create a significant amount of suffering for ourselves:

1. **Our memories are inaccurate**
   They are absolutely unreliable as a reference point. Try it out and ask some friends about a past experience that you share. You will hear different versions of the same story. Try it again a few years later and the stories will differ even more. Every time you think about these inaccurate versions

of the past you bring them back into your current reality. You unconsciously try to recreate the past, only that which once was is already gone. It's no longer here anymore. Your Identified Mind holds on to something virtual, and that creates a feeling of lack.

2. Our imaginings are inadequate

Whatever you imagine to happen in the future, whatever you expect your future to be like... it is highly inadequate! It's nothing but a guessing game prone to create disappointment. Even if you accidentally hit your prediction, you exclude infinite other possible realities. By focussing on one version of the future that your Identified Mind thinks

is pleasant for you, you may block out what is truly nurturing. That which provides real growth cannot be thought of because it is unknown. Only what is already known can be projected. These projections are, by their very nature, limited.

As mentioned earlier, there is no escaping the present moment. **You simply cannot NOT Be Here Now. However virtually you can be all over the place.** By observing habitual tendencies you can burst the virtual bubble and return to the present moment. We'll get there in just a moment but let's sum all this up first.

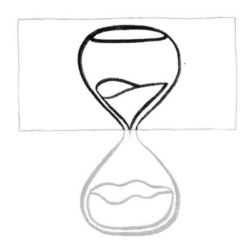

1. Reminiscing

»In the past my life was much easier. There was more freedom, better health and I was a happier person.« The bigger the gap between your memory and the present moment, the more you suffer emotions like guilt and regret.

2. Imagining

»Once I buy that I'll be happy. Five more years until I retire – then I'll enjoy life fully.« The bigger the gap between imagination of the future and the present moment, the more you suffer emotions like anxiety and stress.

3. Distracting

Even if you don't think about the past or the future, your Identified Mind loves to grasp at all kinds of distractions to escape the present moment: »I've got a new message on my phone. Look at how awful these people behave.«

4. Here and now

The only way to experience more presence is to stop escaping into your thoughts. When your full attention is anchored in the now, do you feel any lack? Is there anything missing to be happy? Where is the suffering here and now?

The potential of the present moment
EVERYTHING IS ALREADY HERE

Why even bother to live in the here and now? Here are a few examples that illustrate the potential of the present moment:

- You're a surfer and the crest of a nice sized wave is lifting you up. You're riding down into the barrel in perfect balance. The spray hits your face as you touch the water. You're one with the now.

- You're an architect pitching for a big project. In the presentation you totally forget what you prepared. You have no idea where your words come from but they are perfectly on point. The audience is in awe as you deliver the presentation of your life.

- You're a child chasing butterflies and dancing around the flower garden in the sun.

Some call it flow experience when the idea of time ceases to exist and you're fully absorbed in the present moment. Some call it meditation when you fall in love with what simply is.

When your full attention is anchored in the now, there is NO TIME for lack. There is nothing missing to be happy and there is no room for suffering.

Now, how to get there? You are already there! The only way to bring it more fully into your direct experience is to stop escaping it.

Reroute your attention by persistently bringing it back to the present moment. For adults that may take some practice.

One way is to concentrate on something that just happens naturally, like your breath. There is no need to think about it, no need to generate or interfere. Breathing just happens. By focusing on it your attention is automatically rerouted to the now.

Another way is being very attentive to simple actions like cutting vegetables or intentionally slow-walking step by step out in nature. The attention is narrowed down onto something that happens right now.

If you don't know how to »do« it, ask a small child. If they hurt themselves and see something awe-inspiring right after, the pain is gone. It's flushed out of their attention. If they want ice-cream, they want it now and not tomorrow. What is tomorrow anyway? Small children are mind-emptiness-masters.

All resistance to what simply is needs to dissolve to become fully absorbed in the present moment. This is constantly overlooked because of the astounding simplicity.

Practice what's already here

It seems quite odd to practice being in the present moment when you're always in the midst of it. For the Identified Mind it's even a scary thing to think of: Being swallowed and rendered useless by something that is already here. But that's exactly the point. The Identified Mind itself is causing the separation. Time is thought.

The strategy of these exercises is to cut out distractions, break cycles of habitual mind-patterns and be fully involved with what is.

This involvement is what quite literally leaves no time for anything else. Enjoy cutting vegetables and chasing butterflies!

Top of your lungs
JOYFULLY NOW

1

Whether it's in the shower or in the car, put on your favorite song and sing along at the top of your lungs! The more you impersonate and even dramatize your performance, the more attention is absorbed in the present moment. Even if you're the worst singer on the planet it doesn't matter. Don't hold anything back! This is an assignment.

Digital detox
INTERRUPT THE PHOTON-FIRE

Take vacations from your TV, your computer and your phone. For one day, release yourself from the grip of your screens altogether. If your job doesn't allow that, do it on a weekend. Observe what happens inside you. Are there certain habits and tendencies? Is there anything missing? Are you more aware of the unfolding of the present moment right in front of you?

2

No labels
YOUR MOST NATURAL SEEING

Go out for a walk in nature. A remote place where you don't cross the paths with many people works best. Observe how your Identified Mind constantly and automatically labels everything that you perceive: Tree, leaves, green, bark, bird, sweet and so on. **Bring your attention back to essential perceiving any time you observe a label arise. Let the labels pass.**

3

Notes and reflections

Use this space to draw some patterns. Concentrate to draw them in the way you want and leave no room for thought. You're simply drawing.

»I got it, but...« — Common blocks

»I get distracted all the time. When I try to meditate or focus on my breath, other thoughts come up and I'm gone. How can I combat this distraction?«

»If I stop making plans I'll end up in a really bad spot. I don't have anything to look forward to. I have to think about my future, no?«

Is it you who is gone or just your mind wandering off? You seem to be perfectly clear on what's happening with you. If you'd be gone, who could make an assessment like this? You are not the thinker but the observer of your thoughts. **Don't force it. Just gently bring your attention back into the moment as soon as you become aware that your Identified Mind has gone astray.**
→ See chapter on Monkey-Mind [73]

Thinking about your future doesn't take you anywhere. **Making plans is a practical necessity, nothing bad about that. Just give a little space for spontaneity.** Be aware that every plan is created out of what you already know, and what you already know is stale. This way, you deprive yourself of being surprised by life and making big leaps. Plan, move, intuit, adjust and move on in your own flow.

»I'm here now, done. Now what to do? Just being is totally boring, isn't it? What's next?«

Just being is totally boring for who? It's your Identified Mind speaking there. It's trying to sell you into thinking again. **If you're completely blissfully absorbed in the now, a question like »what's next?« simply does not arise.** As soon as you become aware of your mind's tricks, you're already back in the present moment. Whether to follow and believe a thought or let it float by and relish it. That's up to you.

Got a burning question? Send an email to
Book@MathiasFritzen.com

Head to Heart

FALLING IN LOVE WITH THE MYSTERY OF LIFE
AND RADIATING COMPASSION AND LOVE
THROUGH RADICAL ACCEPTANCE AND SURRENDER.

Truth and Love go together

ABOUT FALLING IN LOVE WITH THE MYSTERY OF LIFE

The argument could be made that the chapter in this book that repels you most is probably the one you should look into the deepest. For many head-centered people, this might be the following chapter. Take heart! There's no way around it.

We easily spend 15+ years in school. An average person reads 120 books in a lifetime – that's around 10.800.000 words. We spend more than 10 years (5.256.000 minutes) in front of a screen watching shows or scrolling through social media time-lines. The density of information that our minds deal with on a daily basis is immense and continues to increase at an exponential rate. How far has all this knowledge taken us in the pursuit of lasting freedom and innermost happiness? Not very far. I advocate for a pause.

A break from ever increasing information intake in order to remember a space deep within yourself that may have faded into obscurity: your heart.

In the Journey chapter I described Truth and Love being two sides of the same coin. **The shift of your vantage point from your Identified Mind back to your Essential Self is Truth. The expression and radiance of this Truth back into the world is Love.**

Let me word it from the perspective of seeking: There is no way around your heart on the way to Self-Realization. This realization moves from head to heart to the beyond. Whatever might be there, hidden in the darkest corners of yourself will come to light. It must in order for you to be fully available to life. How to fall in love with life itself? Through radical acceptance.

Even if you're a high IQ verbal acrobat and whatnot, you know deep within that you can't fake it. If there's something there – a heaviness, a trigger, something bubbling under the surface – you can't fool yourself. If you're radically honest and sincere enough to face what's there, the Journey will take you back into your heart. It will force the attempts of your Identified Mind into submission. It will have you on your knees in the most compassionate way – to remind you of your true nature. To remind you that you are Love.

If all that sounds scary to you, let me ask you: To whom? Who is scared by the prospect of exposure and vulnerability? Who is scared of reconnecting to Love?

Maybe you've heard of this quote taken from a course in miracles: »**Nothing real (your Essential Self) can be threatened. Nothing unreal (your Identified Mind) exists.**«

1. I see you

When you let go of your own perspectives and projections, you begin seeing others for who they truly are for the first time. You realize, that you were projecting a made-up version of reality onto them – your own labels and judgments.

2. I understand you

Radical honesty and sharing from the I-perspective opens up doors for authentic meeting. Your weaknesses and their weaknesses, your strengths and their strengths – you start seeing yourself in the other.

3. I feel you

Feeling someone means letting go of your Identified Mind and remembering your capacity to empathize with another person's momentary experience. The boundaries between the sense of you and other begin to dissolve.

4. I am you

True compassion and unconditional Love cannot be learned or practiced. It is your natural expression once the sense of separation has melted into oneness. How can I not understand and love you if we are essentially one?

10 meditations on the heart

TUNING IN TO THE HEART'S NATURE

You cannot teach a child how to ride a bike by explaining it conceptually. You cannot learn from a book how to kiss and you cannot prepare for falling in love.

Only when something is directly experienced is its essence truly understood and known. Embodiment is the absence of a concept. The concept simply dissolves into intuitive doing. This is moving from head to heart. Don't try to understand, instead meditate on:

1. Mystery

Admit that you don't truly know a single thing. That puts aside the mind and opens your heart to the unknown.

2. Grace

By Grace you were born. By Grace you wake up each morning. By Grace you'll lose your (Identified) mind. Actively invite Grace into your life. It's heart-opening.

3. Acceptance

Radical self-acceptance is the gateway to freedom. It's the end of »I want myself to be different.« aka the end of self-imposed suffering. You are already whole.

4. Forgiveness

Holding grudges is pointless. It recreates the past by transporting it into the now. Forgiveness releases bound negative energy.

5. Surrender

God, life, Truth, your Essential Self – sur-render to the highest principle that speaks to you. May it swallow you completely!

6. Devotion

Devote your whole existence to your high-est priority instead of dividing yourself.

7. Compassion

People are the way they are for a reason. Learn to hold their perspectives. They are equally true or untrue, just like your own.

8. Selflessness

Selflessness is either a fanciful concept or

the absence of your Identified Mind as a living reality. Aim for the latter.

9. Unconditional love

Unconditional love s the logical and utmost natural consequence of oneness. You beat a dog, you beat the one. You make love to your partner, you make love to the one.

10. Absolute involvement

Radically accepting reality as it is right in front of you removes rejection. If rejection is removed, the door is open for involve-ment. Get yourself fully involved in all areas of your life.

Moving from Head to Heart

»Water? What are you talking about?« says the fish. »Love? What are you talking about?« says the Identified Mind. »I can't feel it!«

Take a leap outside of the mind-bubble and know that the whole universe supports your Journey. Your heart is already here, silently waiting for you to wake up and remember.

Truly, you are a master at heart with a beginner's mind. Approach the following exercises with that kind of mindset. To the rational folks out there: This is an assignment that's not up for discussion. It leads to scientifically measurable improvements of your wellbeing.

1

Gratefulness
GIVING RISE TO FULFILLMENT

Every morning, for one week, start your day with a gratitude journal. Write down 3 things/situations/experiences for which you are grateful. After that, take time to sit in silence with each of the three points and **tune into the specific feeling that you associate with that gratitude. Let that beautiful feeling sink in. Soak it up and carry it into your day.**

The taxi-driver
CREATING A NEW REALITY

2

How do you meet and treat the
taxi-driver, your co-worker and your
neighbor? Take up their perspective
on life and see how deeply you can
empathize with their situation. In
your next encounter, **meet them with
freshness and compassion. How can
you make their life-experience wonderful? Exceed your own expectations
in serving them – no strings attached.**

Tonglen
TAKING AND SENDING

3

You can practice Tonglen as a sitting
or walking meditation. **With every
in-breath, visualize inhaling the pain
and suffering of yourself and others.
With every out-breath, visualize sending out what will bring healing to that
suffering.** Practice to heal selfishness
and develop sensitivity and care for
yourself and others. Make the taking
in and sending out bigger.

123

Notes and reflections

Use this space for the gratitude journal and fill it with the most magnificent things, situations and experiences.

»I got it, but...« — Common blocks

»No matter what I do, I can't feel anything. I feel like a stone. How can I connect to my emotions?«

»This whole heart topic is too wishy-washy to me. I want to know more specifically what it's good for and what to do.«

The body is an amazing tool to connect to your emotions. If this book is yoga for the mind, there is also yoga for the body which is what I'd recommend. **Do something physical that shakes up your energies, like dancing, martial arts, rock climbing or yoga.** Leave no room for the mind to enter and be completely involved with movement. Feel what comes up inside of you during these sessions.

Who wants to know that? Your Identified Mind is getting in the way! Your heart doesn't raise doubts like that, wouldn't you agree? From the perspective of your Identified Mind this is a leap of faith straight into the unknown. Dare to lay down your mind for even just a moment. You can pick it back up at any time. It will be right there waiting for you. no worries.
→ See chapter on Monkey-Mind [73]

»It feels like we're getting right back into religious practices and dogmas here. That's not what I was looking for.«

All of these are simple tools and pointers. The responsibility lies with you to pick and choose. It's on you to decide which challenge to take on and when. If you realize your Essential Self without using this book at all, my heart rejoices! Countless paths lead to oneness. Accessible Truth exists beyond doubts and beliefs, beyond concepts and religion.

→ See chapter on 10 warnings [158]

Got a burning question? Send an email to
Book@MathiasFritzen.com

Toolbox

A SET OF USEFUL BITS AND PIECES
TO SUPPORT YOU RESOLVE BLOCKAGES, MAKE DECISIONS,
GET DIRECTIONS AND CREATE NEW PERSPECTIVES.

Mission statement

A QUICK WAY TO GET DIRECTIONS WHEN YOU FEEL STUCK

Answer the following questions. After doing
this, complete the sentences on the right.

1. **Highest Excitement**

   If you can choose only one thing, situation
   or experience: What do you want to have
   the most in your life right now?

2. **Unique Talent**

   Think about your abilities, talents and gifts:
   What is the greatest among them?

3. **Instant Action**

   Which action can you take immediately to
   create a healthier, more expansive, more
   joyful life for yourself?

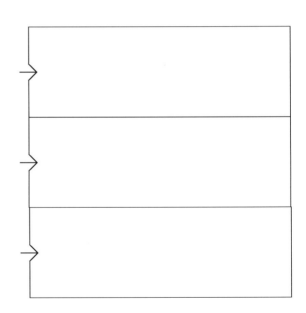

I will do

3. Instant Action

using my

2. Unique Talent

in order to achieve

1. Highest Excitement

Accept or change
THE SIMPLICITY OF DECISION-MAKING

No matter what life-situation you're unhappy with, essentially you've got only two options: Accept or change. Often times we do neither and stay in the gray-zone in between — not fully accepting the situation as it is but also not changing it wholeheartedly. This limbo is what causes tremendous amounts of suffering.

Think of a situation that you're unhappy with and ask yourself: Am I in full acceptance? It is useful to work through the chapter on → Radical Honesty [45] to be able to answer this question truthfully for yourself. Obviously the answer is »No, I am not.« otherwise you wouldn't be unhappy in the first place. Full acceptance and letting go are the same thing.

Full acceptance means to surrender entirely to what simply is. Can you do that?

If you can't, the other option comes into play: Change. You figured out that you cannot accept the situation as it is, so it's time to take action and change it. Don't be afraid to break it down — »I'm not happy with my marriage« doesn't necessarily mean to leave it. Once you work through the chapter on → Intuition [29] you'll most likely already know what to do. If not, revisit the chapter on → Be Here Now [101] and see what comes up in this very moment. **It's time for self-responsibility. You are in charge! For how much longer are you willing to stay in the limbo and suffer? Accept or change.**

Thought-replacement

FLUSHING OUT NEGATIVE THOUGHT-PATTERNS AND REWIRING YOUR BRAIN

Your attitude towards life defines how you act. The emotional state that you're in has a great influence on your attitude. Emotions are rooted in thoughts. Some of these thoughts are conscious, others are unconscious. However, there is a core-thought for every undesirable state that you may find yourself in.

Having worked through this book you know already that you're not the thinker of your thoughts, but the observer. Every thought comes and goes. You watch it and you have the choice to give it your attention or not. You decide whether to believe it or not. Yet, some thoughts can be very sticky. Here's a great tool to inquire deeper and to actively replace them.

Draw a spreadsheet like the exemplary one you see on the next page, choose a situation that you feel stuck in and fill in the left column first. You can start in any of the three rows.

Now replace your core-thought with an extraordinarily positive one. How would you feel when thinking that new thought? How would you act when feeling that new emotion?

Nothing in this world has one single inherent meaning. There are countless perspectives for every situation. **Why would you not choose to think this new, positive thought instead? Cultivate it! Over time you can literally rewire your brain.**

Current Situation

Desired Outcome

Thought

Others look down on me and don't accept me for who I am.

Others want to be around me. They love me for who I am.

Emotion

I feel worthless and alone.

I feel seen, appreciated and loved.

Action

I hide. If I go out I mind-read and try to fulfill expectations. I try to be someone that I am not.

I am free to be myself wherever I go. My actions are content and come from a place of lightness.

135

Attitude-assessment

FIND OUT ABOUT YOUR CURRENT STATE AND WHAT LIES BEYOND

1. Body-centered-state

An unconscious and contracted state with a very active Identified Mind. It's perceived that life happens TO YOU and you have no say about it. Common descriptors are: Inactivity, passivity, anxiety, doubtfulness and conflict.

→ See chapter on Radical Honesty [45]

2. Mind-centered-state

A more energetic state with an Identified Mind in productivity-mode. It's perceived that life happens directly BY YOU and that you are in charge. Common descriptors are: Action, change, movement but also excess and attachment to your own productions.

→ See chapter on Mirroring [87]

3. Heart-centered-state

A conscious, open and positive state with a quiet Identified Mind. It's perceived that life happens THROUGH YOU for the greater good of all. Common descriptors are: Peace, harmony, joy, intelligence and compassion.

→ See chapter on Head to Heart [115]

4. Beyond

The dissolving of the Identified Mind into loving presence and the permanent recognition of ever present awareness as your own self. This leads to a stateless-state in which all the other states appear in harmony. Common descriptors are: Non-judgment, unconditional love and wisdom.

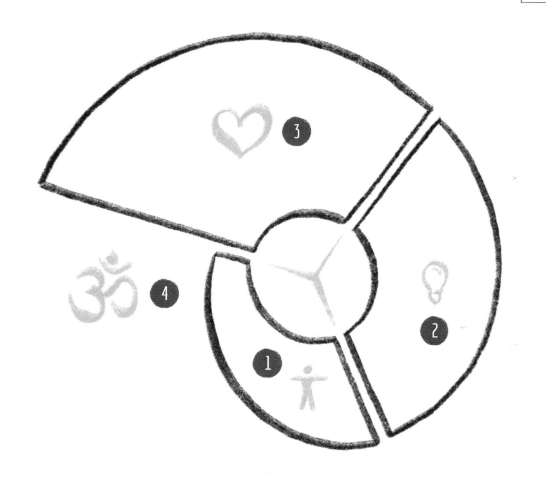

Subconscious mind

FLASH-FROZEN CONSCIOUSNESS

Everything is consciousness and the subconscious mind contains flash-frozen bits and pieces of that same consciousness.

When you're facing an emotionally tough situation that you can't handle in that moment, your mind has a built-in security-measure. It freezes the situation and dumps it away »under water«. Of course it's still there lingering, but at least for that moment of crisis it's out of sight. Let me be clear, that's a good thing!

Metaphorically speaking it's like an iceberg. What you're conscious of sits above the water line and what you're unconscious of lies below. On days when the water becomes clearer you might get a glimpse of that part of yourself that exists below the surface.

Every now and then parts of your deeper layers come to the surface. It happens at exactly the right time – when you are ready to face it, learn the respective lesson and integrate it into your life. What used to be unknown is no longer a scary »other«.

The more you become aware of your own subconscious fragments, the more you start seeing similar tendencies in others. You can empathize, relate and connect to others more easily and more deeply until all becomes one.

Paradoxes

THE UNIVERSE HAS A SENSE OF HUMOR

One of my favorite paradoxical questions when I was a kid: »Can God create a stone that's so heavy that he cannot lift it by himself?«

One of my favorite poems by Rumi still is: »I have lived on the lip of insanity, wanting to know reasons, knocking on a door. It opens. I've been knocking from the inside.«

Something means this AND that at the same time. It has multiple meanings, like light being a wave and a particle, depending on how you look at it. There is no consensus of what we call consensus-reality. Reality is self-contradictory as long as you stay in this physical realm. Investigation leads to logically unac-ceptable conclusions and that's something absolutely wonderful! It's like an unpredictable dance of the quantum-field.

Take hypothesis C: Cats always land on their feet. Combine it with hypothesis B: Buttered toast always lands buttered side down. You've got a flying cat and invented anti-gravity! Not.

If you think you know one thing: that you know nothing... then perhaps if I'm very quiet I can hear your one-hand clapping.

Circle of life
WHEEL OF FORTUNE

This is a little poetic, so follow me freeflow:

From a state of oneness [1] in the center of the illustration we grow into our identifications [2]. Slowly the Identified Mind assembles itself. In expanding cycles [3] we grow up, revisiting the same places again from time to time to meet the respective lessons in a deeper, more meaningful way.

We move into the world more and more [4] and the interrelated opposites – the Ying and Yang – cycle around each other like the double helix of our DNA. At the peak of our egoic expression [5], when we think we know a whole lot and have most things figured out, the tension of our self-made illusion becomes intolerable. A critical point is reached and consciousness folds back on itself. We start to look within and slowly begin to remember and return to our Essential Self [6]. It dawns on us that all identifications are just part of a play that we witness [7].

Ying and Yang coil around each others in their natural way with increasing frequency [8]. Whirling in ever smaller circles as we close in on oneness once again. This time however, we're conscious of it [9]. Birth and death are just points of transition [10], necessary to experience our Essential Self in physical form.

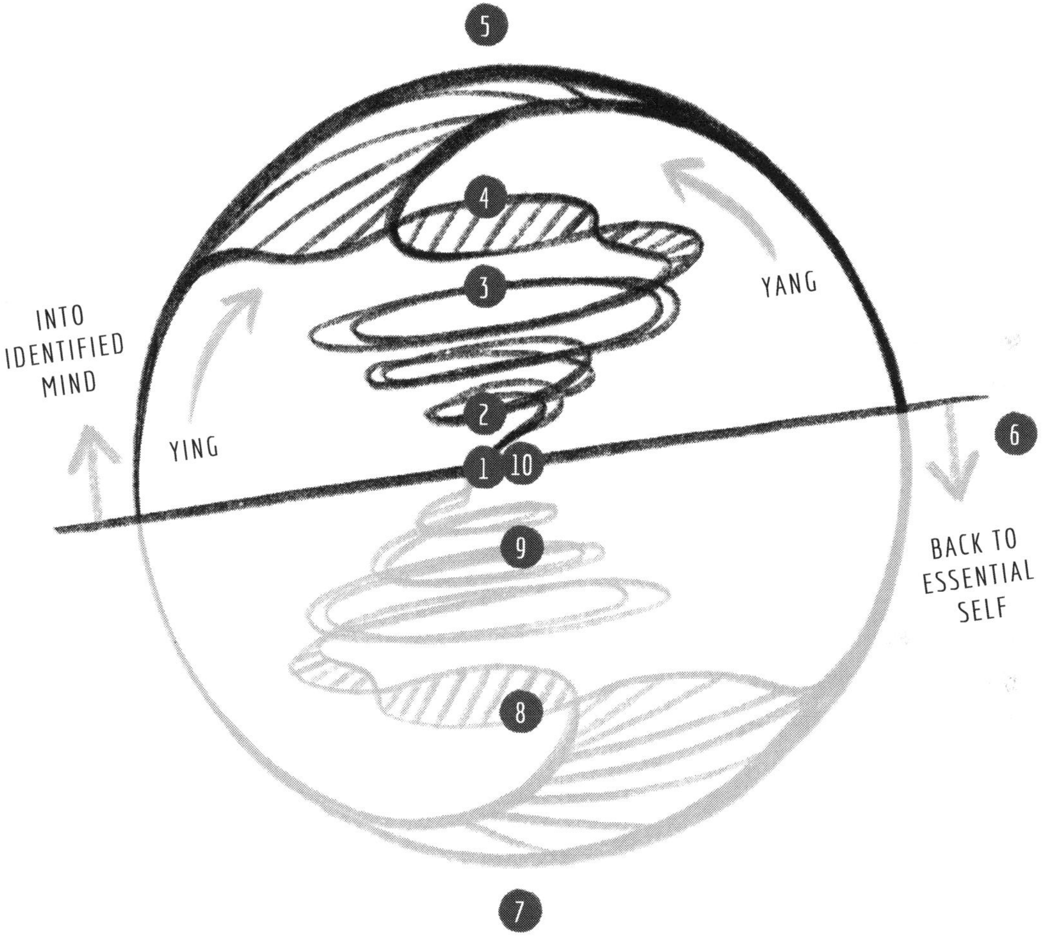
5
4
3
2
1
10
6
9
8
7
INTO
IDENTIFIED
MIND
YING
YANG
BACK TO
ESSENTIAL
SELF

Backtracing perspectives

EVERYTHING YOU WILL EVER KNOW IS ALREADY HERE

You are behind the telescope observing count-less stars in an infinite universe. That's the common perspective. A small separate entity hoping for another small separate entity to exist on a planet far away. An ET peering into the telescope as well to finally, one lucky day, meet with you for an interstellar drink.

Now let me ask you a question: Have you ever experienced anything outside of yourself? Contemplate this deeply. Everything you perceive, sense and experience has happened, happens and will happen within you, right?

You are aware of the stars and the telescope at the same time. You are aware of your body standing behind it looking through the lens. You are aware of what you touch, taste, hear, smell and see in this moment. You are aware of emotions that come up. You are aware of your thoughts. You are aware of the thinker of your thoughts.

Everything that you can perceive is an object of your perception that appears in front of you. So you must be the subject!

If you are the subject and what you perceive is objects the implication is: whatever you per-ceive cannot be you.

Shifting perspectives

EXAMINING YOUR VANTAGE-POINT FURTHER

See the dot on the next page? Let's say that's you. A tiny human on a small blue planet; circling around a little sun somewhere in the outer region of a spiral galaxy called milky way. A finite bit of consciousness somewhere in an infinite universe (represented by the space around the dot). That's you in the common perspective.

You are the dot. The universe is the space.

But what if it's the other way around? You are infinite conscious awareness and the universe is a speck of dust appearing within you. You are the space and the universe is the dot.

On the last page I mentioned that everything appears within you as an object of your perception. It is the same here. The entire universe (or multiverse, if you want) appears within you.

How to find out if it's actually true? If what you really are is infinite conscious awareness, it must be possible to experience it beyond any doubt. What you are must be experience-able, right? That's how to find out if what I say is true or not. In fact, that's the only way to find out – through your direct experience.

This is what the shifting vantage point from your Identified Mind to your Essential Self does: You swap seats with the universe.

Roadmap of Self-Realization

MACRO AND MICRO TOOLS FOR POSITIONING

The purpose of this Roadmap is to give a rough orientation where you are in the process and in doing so reduce confusion. My suggestion: Orient yourself but don't hold onto it.

If you never feel the urge to look at this Roadmap at all, that's perfectly OK too. In fact you're taking a risk looking at it. It's food for your Identified Mind that it might try to grasp at. Simply be aware of that.

Everyone moves at their own pace and sequence. Some can evolve simultaneously. You see, there's no general recipe here. It also wouldn't be as much fun. You're in the right place at the right time.

With a little creativity you can use this Roadmap in two ways:

Macro: Assess where you are in the greater scheme of Self-Realization.

Micro: Assess where you are within a smaller growth-cycle, like »I'm practicing radical honesty with myself.«

On the following pages you'll find the 10 segments of the circle explained in detail.

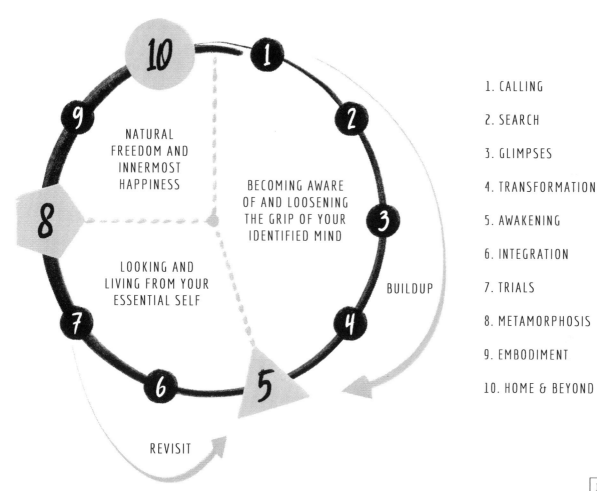

1. CALLING

2. SEARCH

3. GLIMPSES

4. TRANSFORMATION

5. AWAKENING

6. INTEGRATION

7. TRIALS

8. METAMORPHOSIS

9. EMBODIMENT

10. HOME & BEYOND

❶ Calling

There's more to life and I can feel it. I don't know what it is and I can't explain it, but I can no longer ignore the pull. The calling to find Truth initiates my search.

I am this body, mind and identity.	I realize that there is more to life and that it's different from what I've known so far.
My practice is courageously taking the first steps.	My challenge is that I often get sidetracked from what I truly want.

❷ Search

The search is full on. **I'm ready to drop my old ways and perspectives and I'm opening up for the unknown.** Hints and traces are guiding me, sometimes in mysterious ways.

I am this body and mind.	I realize that what I thought to be true is relative or even illusory.
My practice is strengthening the connection to my Intuition.	My challenge is that my mind interprets and labels everything that I experience.

Glimpses

 Transformation

Experientially I get glimpses of deep peace, great joy, a sense of bliss and new found freedom. Undeniably I'm headed in the right direction.

Everything in my life changes: They way I perceive things, the way I think and interact. It's like I'm being reinvented from inside out. I play an active part and I watch it unfold.

I am much more than this body and mind.

I realize that I'm knee deep into discovering something profound.

My practice is letting go of old ways and surrendering to the new.

My challenge is,that I constantly drop in and out of this new sense of me.

I am my Intuition and my heart.

I realize that I'm growing into a new and more essential sense of me.

My practice is to confirm my realizations in everyday-life.

My challenge is that I get triggered all the time and now I'm aware of it.

151

5 Awakening

I experience who I truly am. All objects of perception cease to exist – there is only the subject experiencing itself. What I was looking for is where I'm looking from: 180° shift.

I am consciousness.	I realize that the search led me astray and that I was always already THAT.
My practice is no practice, since all practice is drained of meaning.	My challenge is that my mind wants to catch hold of this experience and make it its own.

6 Integration

I know who I am now but I'm still moving in the same world. **Somehow I'm in this world but not of it.** This new way of seeing needs to be integrated thoroughly.

I am consciousness in motion.	I realize that this profound shift in perspective needs to sink in.
My practice is to create space for the delicate alignment of the new seeing.	My challenge is that old ways don't work anymore and I'm not used to the new ones yet.

 Trials

Life is testing out the solidity of my realization. There are plenty of situations where I have the option to meet it in the old or the new way. It's up to me, and that requires vigilance.

I am confused.	I realize that I know nothing at all and what I hold onto is taken away.
My practice is to get back to my practice and to trust deeply.	My challenge is that problems resurface with which I thought I was done.

8 Metamorphosis

There really is no reference point here. Center-less living in the moment. The contractions of trial and integration seep out and the dust of confusion settles. It was all just birth pain.

I am pure awareness.	I realize the simplicity of being.
My practice is life.	My challenge is that there is no reference-point anymore.

9 Embodiment

The old ways have been rendered useless and **I naturally meet life from the place of my Essential Self.** Every step is taking place in uncharted territory. Every breath is unique.

I am nothing and everything.	I realize that the path from the highest mountaintop leads back to the marketplace of the world.
My practice is to honor and hold the equilibrium.	My challenge is that this is walking in uncharted territory.

10 Home & Beyond

This is just utterly simple. One could say it's the magnificent ordinariness in every detail that catches my attention. Words don't apply... Here. Now.

I am free.	I radiate Love and wisdom, compassion and gratefulness
I'm of service.	Your challenge is my challenge.

Self-Realization is swapping seats with the universe.

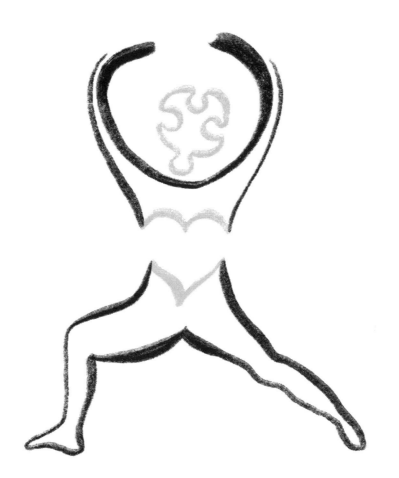

10 warnings

1. **Direct speech**

   I'm addressing you directly in this book to get straight to the point without detours. I will assume that you are approaching this book from a place of not-knowing, like someone who's asking a burning question. However, there may very well be chapters that you have fully realized and integrated already. If that's the case, simply move to the next.

2. **Limits of language**

   The Truth that I'm pointing towards throughout the book is experiential in its nature. Every attempt to put it in words is bound to fall short. This Truth exists outside of concepts and cannot be conceptualized. Yet this is what I'm doing in this book. I'm taking it lightly and hope you do, too.

3. **Identified Mind 2.0**

   The tools I'm offering in this book can lead to great openings for you. The Identified Mind loves that and will most likely try to make these experiences its own. It attaches itself to them in order to re-inflate. All of a sudden you hear yourself talking like the most radically honest person on the planet. You're the one who transcended the Monkey-Mind best. You're Here Now better than anyone else. This is what I call the Identified Mind 2.0 – another illusory bubble.

4. Not a joyride

Self-Realization has two perspectives to it. One being that you remember your Essential Self and relax back into your natural freedom and innermost happiness. Sounds beautiful, and it's the true perspective. However, there is a second side to be aware of – the perspective of your Identified Mind. Self-Realization is discovering the illusory nature of the Identified Mind. It's not hard to imagine that the Identified Mind doesn't like that and wants to avoid it at all costs. Before your perspective has shifted radically you look out from your Identified Mind, so its experience is your experience. Looking from here the shift can feel very disorienting for a while. It leads to significant changes internally and in many cases externally as well. Be aware of that.

5. Not another dogma

I cannot repeat it often enough: What I offer here are pointers and tools. There is no need to believe in them. This is about self-responsibility and your direct experience only. Everything that remains on a level of mere head-knowledge for you is literally worthless. That which becomes undeniably true for you experientially is what you're aiming at. Truth – with a capital T – may sound dogmatic in itself. However, this is your invitation to explore on your own and eventually become the living proof that this Truth exists. The one, all-inclusive, timeless Truth prior to any idea of dogma and religion.

6. Psychedelics

It has become en vogue to experiment with psychedelics these days. It makes sense in a society that likes quick and easy. I've never tried them, but I know quite a few people who have. What I see is that these substances skyrocket you into experiences that want to be integrated once you're eventually back on earth. There are no shortcuts! Don't mistake rockets for a good exploratory hike with a clear mind.

7. The nature of doubt

Zen-masters have a history of discarding questions. Whatever question their students come up with, they know it's coming from the Identified Mind. If for one of the students no questions or doubts arise anymore – something interesting might have happened. I'm over-generalizing, but the point is clear.

8. State-trap

Many have glimpses of the Truth – mystical experiences that can be absolutely extraordinary and blissful. A very common trap is to try and return to that very experience. This attempt is in itself a trap. The

Truth shows itself in many ways and cannot be pinpointed. Furthermore: Self-Realization is not a state! Everything else is a state. Keep that in mind. Or maybe not.

9. Relax a little

Don't stress yourself out. Everything comes exactly at the right time. Where you are is where you're supposed to be. Grasping to arrive somewhere is a trap of the Identified Mind to keep you busy and in limbo.

10. Just a human

Countless times I've ignored my Intuition, in some cases for many years. I always liked the idea of honesty as long as it didn't touch my own vulnerability. I was quite good at finding flaws in others but not in myself. I lived in a mental world most of the time – zoned out from the reality right in front of me. I had many judgments and a very distinct world-view without leaving room for alternatives. My heart was something only few people knew. I've failed again and again, having desires, addictions and ignoring my own dark corners. I'm human and my poop stinks like everyone else's.

Incredibly grateful — Thank you...

Rebecca for your unconditional love and support, for bouncing ideas and finetuning the details. Without you this book wouldn't have been possible. I love you and I bow to you.

Steven, Andrew and so many more for your insightful feedback throughout the writing-process.

Mum and Dad for your inexhaustible support in everything I do. You are wonderful!

Antonia for hosting me in Conil de la Frontera where this book was written. ¡Muchas gracias por su hospitalidad!

To the many teachers and guides that have graced my path throughout the years. Thank you for your reflections – for reminding me of what is true and what is illusion.

Mooji... tears of gratitude stream down my face as I write this. Thank you for your guidance, your patience and your loving presence. Thank you for showing me who I am. Words do not suffice.

Thank you. Thank you. Thank you.

Finally, thank you dear reader for having the balls to look within and trust your Self.

About the author

BY REBECCA ROBERTS

Mathias has had a lifelong Love affair with the search for Truth and deeper understanding of life. From the age of six he recalls experiences that gave a hearty jolt to his way of seeing and experiencing the world. The explorations that followed served to lay the foundations for the work he does today.

As an introverted and somewhat timid child, Martial Arts (especially Kung-Fu) provided a doorway into full expression. He helped bring the sport of Parkour to Germany in 2002 – mind over matter! Exploring old conventions and physical limitations – everything was open to questioning. That permeated even his thesis in digital design, which focused on

Singularity – a point in time where human and machine intelligence merge and technological advancement progresses instantly.

All of these experiences provided insights and learnings, but the questions raised during his childhood would not be appeased simply with external inputs. When this became clear, Mathias turned inward with the same inexhaustible fervor. This led to an exploration beyond conditioning, beyond the mind and identity. The hunger to understand the question »Who am I?« brought him into direct experience and turned his world upside down. In an instant his deepest questions were answered, not by the mind but in a place far truer and deeper.

Mathias now focuses his energy and attention to pointing others towards a deeply intimate connection and Love for Truth. With a mix of compassion and no-bullshit directness, he creates a space which is fertile for transformation.

He currently holds workshops, meetings, retreats and individual 1:1 sessions. All of these have one goal – to be of service to others in shedding the layers of illusory identification in order to reconnect to lasting freedom and innermost happiness.

For more information, please visit
MathiasFritzen.com

Got a burning question?
Send an email to

Book@MathiasFritzen.com

Now forget about all
the concepts in this book.
They are crutches.
It's time to walk freely.

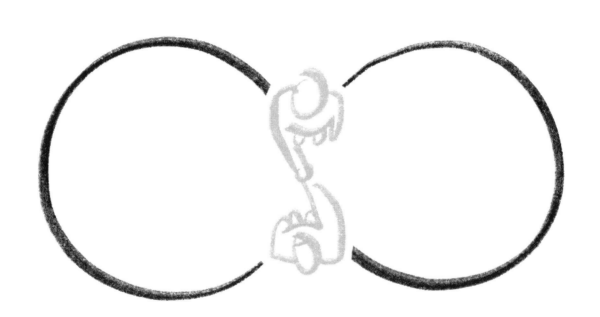

30620473R00108

Printed in Poland
by Amazon Fulfillment
Poland Sp. z o.o., Wrocław